This
Collector's Edition
BELONGS TO

— — — — — — — —

MY Collection of COLLECTIONS

MY Collection of COLLECTIONS

by

Nina Chakrabarti and

- - - - - - - - - - - - -

LAURENCE KING PUBLISHING

Published in 2017
by Laurence King Publishing Ltd
361–373 City Road
London EC1V 1LR
United Kingdom
Tel: +44 20 7841 6900
Fax: +44 20 7841 6910
e-mail: enquiries@laurenceking.com
www.laurenceking.com

A catalog record for this book is available from the British Library.

ISBN: 978-1-78627-061-0

Printed in China

For
Ben Branagan

SOME COLLECTIONS
BELONG in a MUSEUM...

... WHERE they GIVE US A GLIMPSE into THE PAST

OTHERS LIE ABANDONED UNDER *the* BED

OR LOVINGLY STUCK into AN ALBUM

THIS COLLECTION is FROM A RAILWAY LOST and FOUND DEPARTMENT

INVENT a STORY
USING ALL the LOST ITEMS

... like MUGS

ADD
STICKERS ON TO
the PLAIN MUGS...
OR DRAW ON YOUR OWN DESIGN

... or POT PLANTS...

ADD to THE COLLECTION BY DRAWING PLANTS FOR the EMPTY POTS

... or SHOES!

CUSTOMIZE this PAIR

SOME COLLECTIONS are ACCIDENTAL

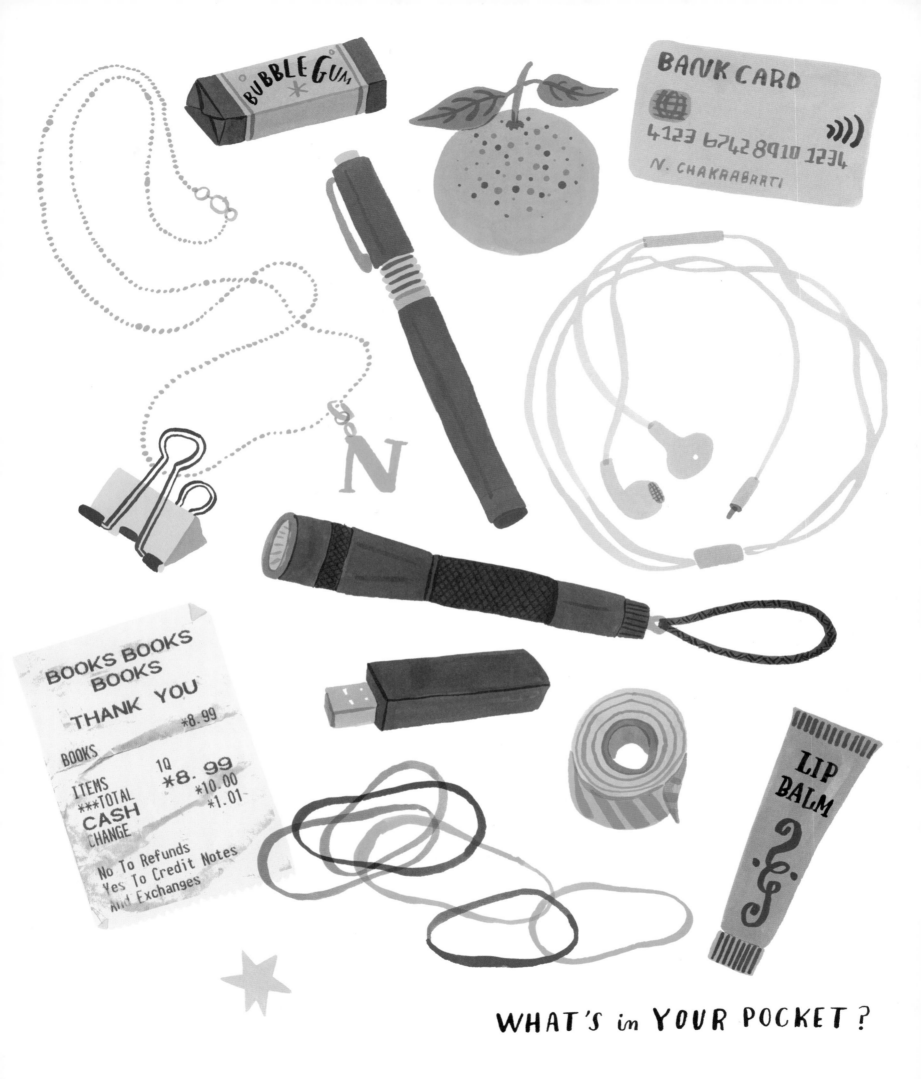

OTHERS are PLANNED CAREFULLY, LIKE AMERICAN POET EMILY DICKINSON'S HERBARIUM

(a HERBARIUM is A COLLECTION of DRIED PLANTS)

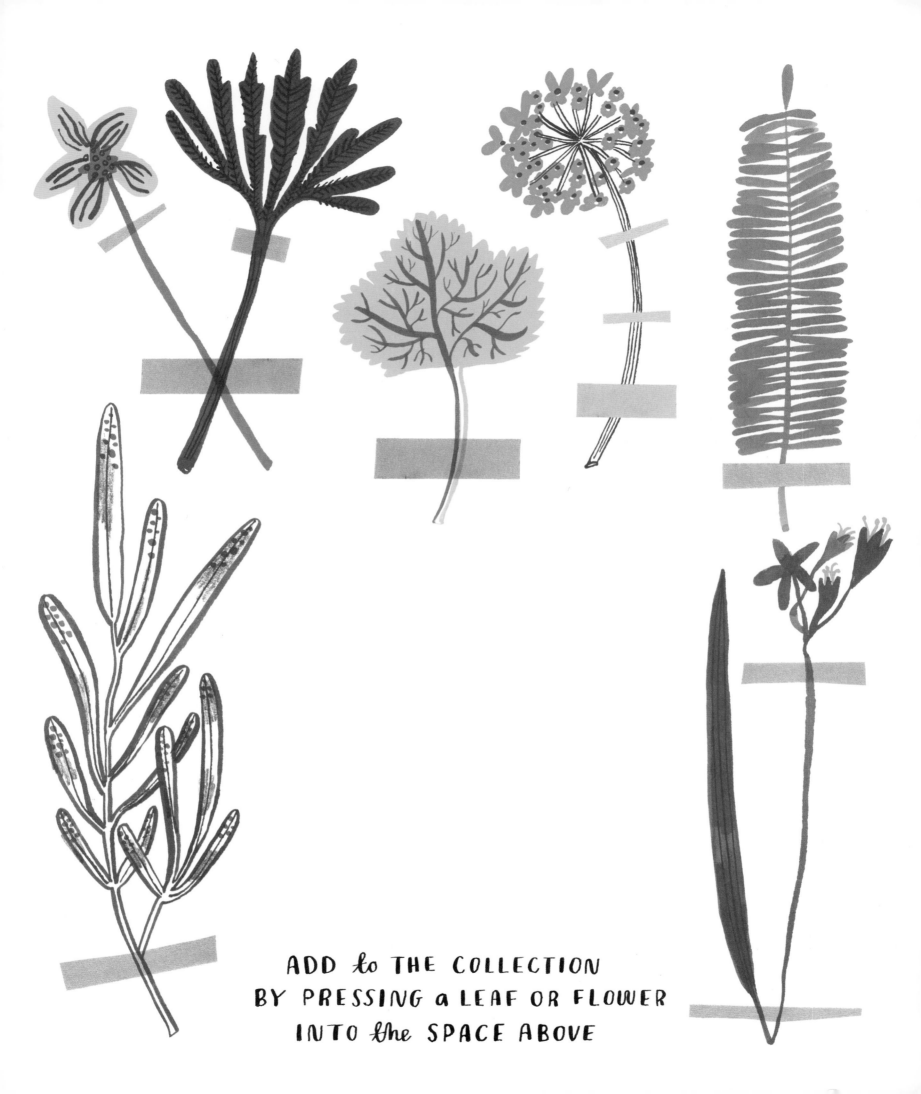

ADD to THE COLLECTION
BY PRESSING a LEAF OR FLOWER
INTO the SPACE ABOVE

PERHAPS YOU'LL START a COLLECTION DEVOTED to JUST ONE PLANT

THESE are ALL LEAVES
FROM DIFFERENT TYPES OF OAK TREE
(THERE are 600 to CHOOSE FROM!)

IF YOU COME ACROSS an OAK LEAF STICK it DOWN HERE

SOME COLLECTIONS are
JUST FOR THE AFTERNOON...

WOODLAND TREASURES
PICKED UP, ADMIRED,
and THEN LEFT FOR OTHER
WALKERS *to* CRUNCH OVER

ADD CLOUDS YOU'VE SEEN
TO THIS COLLECTION

OTHER COLLECTIONS
GROW OVER
many LIFETIMES...

...and ARE STILL GROWING

MAYBE YOU like COLLECTING
ROUND OBJECTS...

USE *this* BIT OF THE PAGE
to ADD MORE ROUND THINGS
TO *the* COLLECTION

...LIKE BADGES...

THE BLANK ONES are FOR YOU to DRAW ON

...or COINS?

ADD YOUR own DESIGNS to THE BLANK COINS

MAKE SOME COIN RUBBINGS HERE

PLACE a COIN UNDER THIS PAGE and GENTLY RUB OVER THE AREA WITH a PENCIL

YEARS ago COWRIE SHELLS
WERE used AS CURRENCY

NOW they MIGHT BE PART of a COLLECTION WASHED UP on a BEACH

HERE is A COLLECTION of GREAT COLLECTORS

Sir Hans Sloane

had a **GIGANTIC** collection of **71,000 RARE** and **EXCEPTIONAL OBJECTS**

Mary Anning
collected **FOSSILS**

King George V
collected **STAMPS**

Augustus Pitt Rivers
collected **ARCHAEOLOGICAL**
and **ETHNOGRAPHIC** artifacts

Sir Henry Wellcome

collected OBJECTS and BOOKS about MEDICINE

Peggy Guggenheim

COLLECTED MODERN ART and LHASA APSO DOGS

Elizabeth Taylor

collected RARE and EXQUISITE jewellery (and HUSBANDS)

YOUR PORTRAIT HERE ↑

COLLECTIONS CAN BE ECLECTIC...

MOON ROCK

AMMONITE FOSSIL

POTTERY FRAGMENT

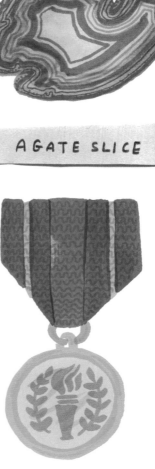

BUTTERFLY WING

BIRD FEATHER

AGATE SLICE

GORILLA-SHAPED STONE

POPPY SEED POD

GLASS EYE

SOY SAUCE

SWIMMING MEDAL

SOCCER STICKERS

SLINGSHOT

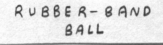

ARROWHEAD

RUBBER-BAND BALL

STAG BEETLE

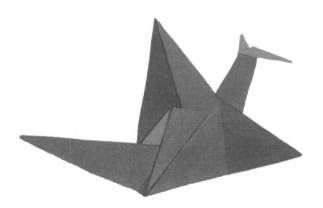

ORIGAMI CRANE

SNAKE STONE

MANY-SIDED DIE

CHARM

SEA URCHIN SHELL

PLASTIC CAMEL

RING PULL

TREASURES BELONGING to RAFI, AGED 11½

... or SPECIFIC to ONE THING ONLY

PERHAPS YOU'RE a
BUTTON COLLECTOR...

Vanilla

Jasmine

Cinnamon

Bubblegum

OR A PERFUMER who COLLECTS SCENTS?

Grass

Bonfire

Seaweed

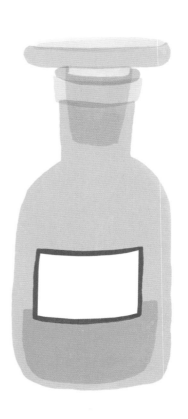

ADD YOUR FAVORITE
SMELL to THE COLLECTION

SUCROLOGISTS COLLECT SMALL PACKETS of SUGAR

COCONUT SUGAR

Suiker
KINKERSTRAAT 112
AMSTERDAM

ZUCCHERO

Natural Brown SUGAR
for the connoisseur's coffee

Sugar
Sugar
Sugar

MEXICANA
AZÚCAR · SUGAR

SUCRE

SUGAR
SUGAR
SUGAR
SUGAR
Pure Sugar

sugar
Зáхарн

Oh Thank Heaven
SUGAR

Zucker

Brown Sugar

LIKE the KIND YOU FIND in CAFÉS AND RESTAURANTS

PHILLUMENISTS COLLECT MATCHBOXES, MATCHBOOKS and MATCHBOX LABELS

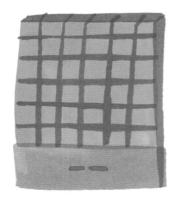

FALERISTS COLLECT MEDALS of ALL KINDS

WHO would YOU HONOR WITH a MEDAL?

FILL each BLANK MEDAL WITH a NAME

SOME COLLECTIONS HAVE a COLOR in COMMON

THESE BLUE OBJECTS HAVE all BEEN COLLECTED by THE SATIN BOWERBIRD

HE LIKES to DECORATE
HIS NEST to IMPRESS
HIS MATE

OTHERS are ABOUT MEMORIES

STORE SPECIAL TICKETS,
PHOTOS, or
OTHER MEMENTOS
in HERE

MY
collection of
MEMORIES

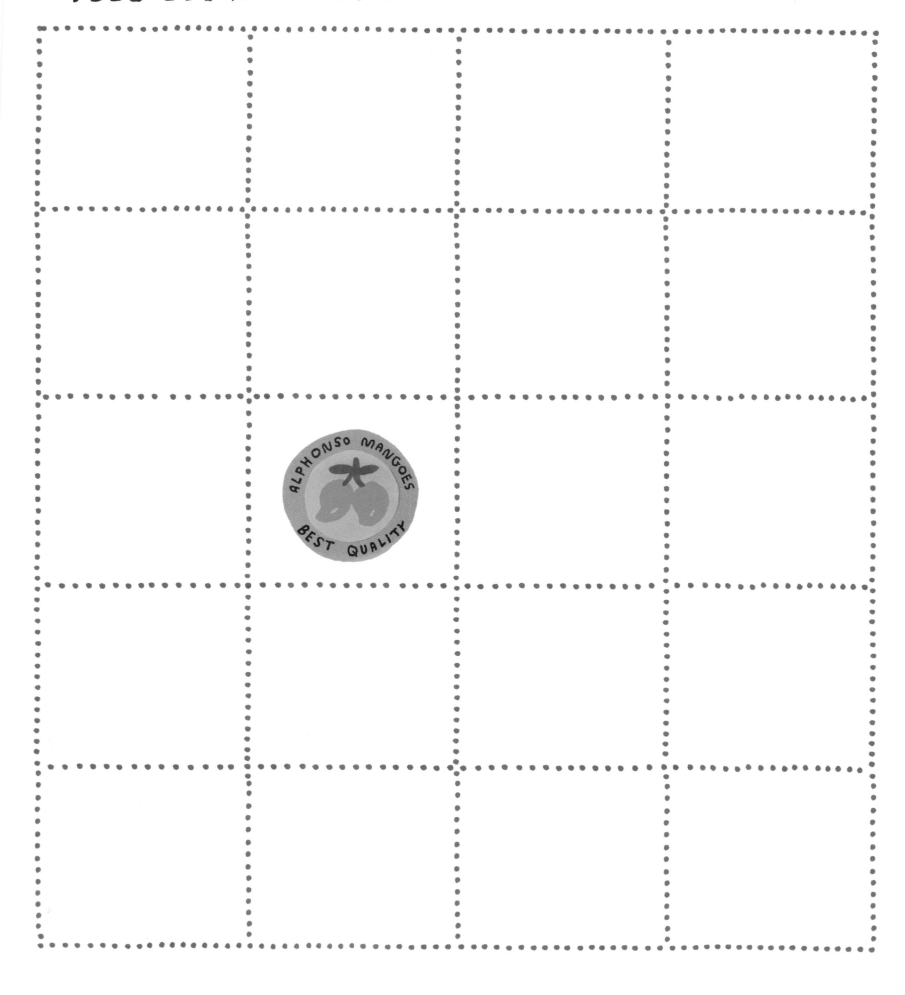

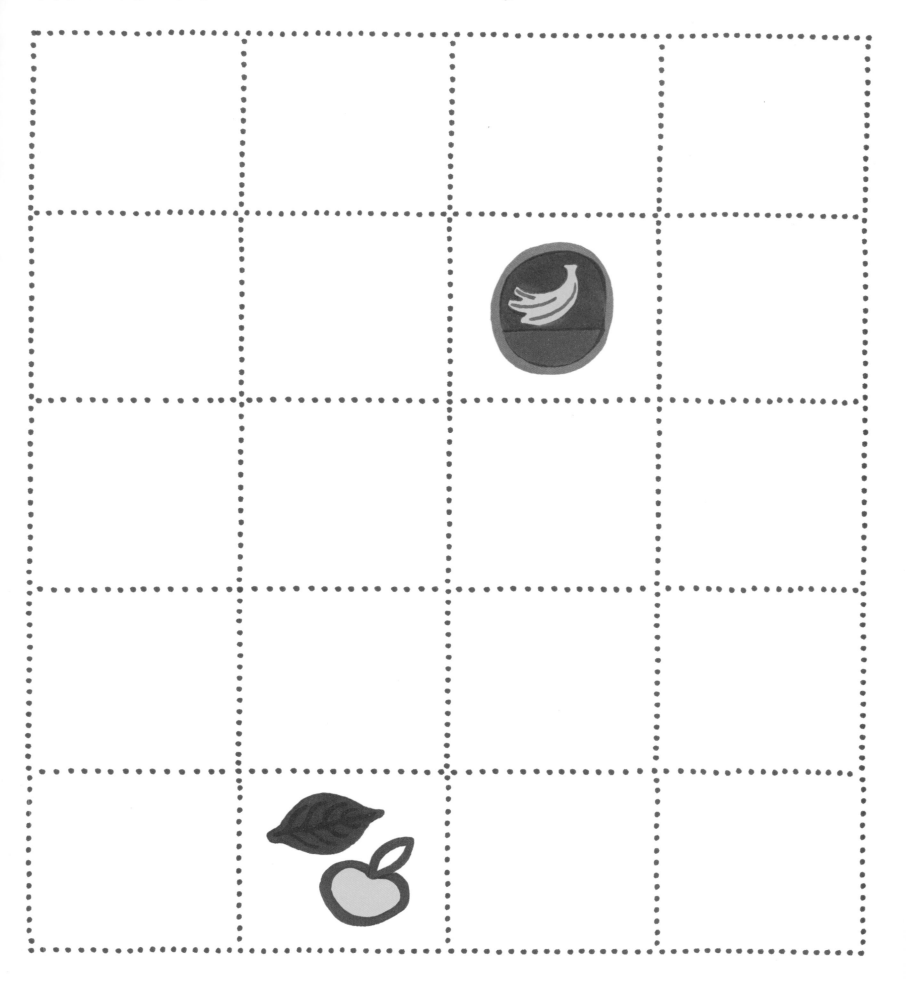

SOME COLLECTIONS are ABOUT SECRETS

'LOVERS' EYES'
were MINIATURE PAINTINGS
DESIGNED to HIDE
A PARAMOUR'S IDENTITY

A COLLECTION CAN COME FROM LOTS of DIFFERENT PLACES...

MEX
MEXICO CITY
FLIGHT NUMBER 54

LON
LONDON
FLIGHT NUMBER
02-30-52

DRAW YOUR OWN LUGGAGE TAG HERE

NEW YORK
NYC
Nº6210

LAX
LOS ANGELES

PAR
PARIS

HND
TOKYO
Nº 4942

BUDAPEST
BUD
FLIGHT
422

93

YYZ
TORONTO

… or IT COULD BE about ONE PLACE

NETSUKE (say 'NET-SOO-KAY') are TINY, CARVED OBJECTS FROM JAPAN THAT HANG FROM the SASH OF a KIMONO

COLLECTIONS are a WAY of UNDERSTANDING THE WORLD we LIVE in...

A WUNDERKAMMER (a cabinet of curiosities)
SHOWCASED RARE and EXOTIC ITEMS
FOR PEOPLE TO MARVEL AT

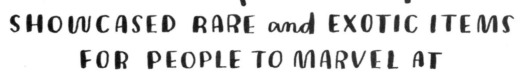

...or A WAY of ENJOYING LANGUAGE

Sassafras

- - - - - - - - - - - - - - - - - - -

Shenanigans
- - - - - - - - -
RAZZMATAZZ

- - - - - - - - - - - -

- - - - - - - - - - - - - - - - -

Perspicacious
MUMBO-JUMBO

- -

WRITE YOUR FAVORITE WORDS
ON the DOTTED LINES

Fantastic ----------------

---------- Biscuit

---------- Periwinkle

TIFFIN ----------------

---------------- Bamboozle

CONSTANTINOPLE

---------- Whiskers

MAKE a POEM USING THE WORDS
ON these PAGES

EVERY COLLECTION STARTS with JUST ONE OBJECT

...and THEN it GROWS...

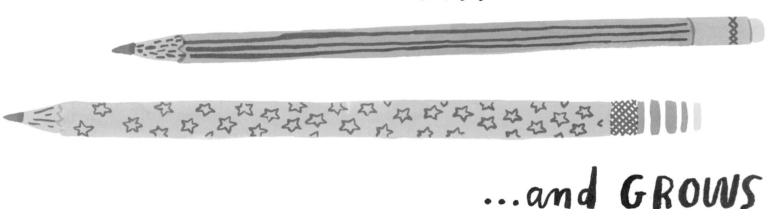

...and GROWS

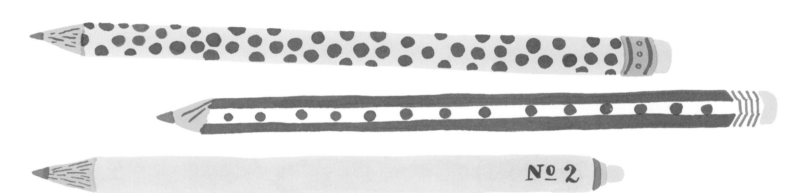

No 2

...and KEEPS on GROWING.

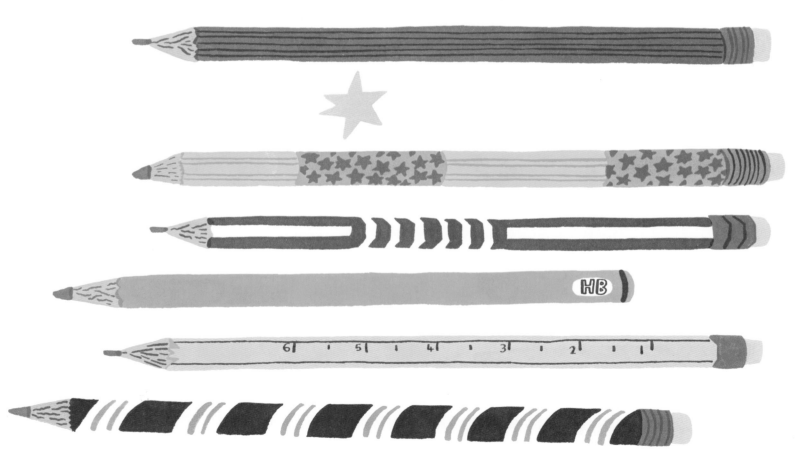

TIME to START YOUR own COLLECTION ...

3263458

130
P
1 Class

DRAW PICTURES, stick THINGS in, or WRITE DESCRIPTIONS of WHAT you WANT to COLLECT!

YOU can ADD these STICKERS in WHERE YOU SEE a ✦ OR simply STICK them WHEREVER YOU want!

60 DANMARK

Thank you!

Laurence King, Jo Lightfoot, Angus Hyland,
Elizabeth Jenner, Chloë Pursey,
Chelsea Edwards, Vanessa Green,
and Ben Branagan.

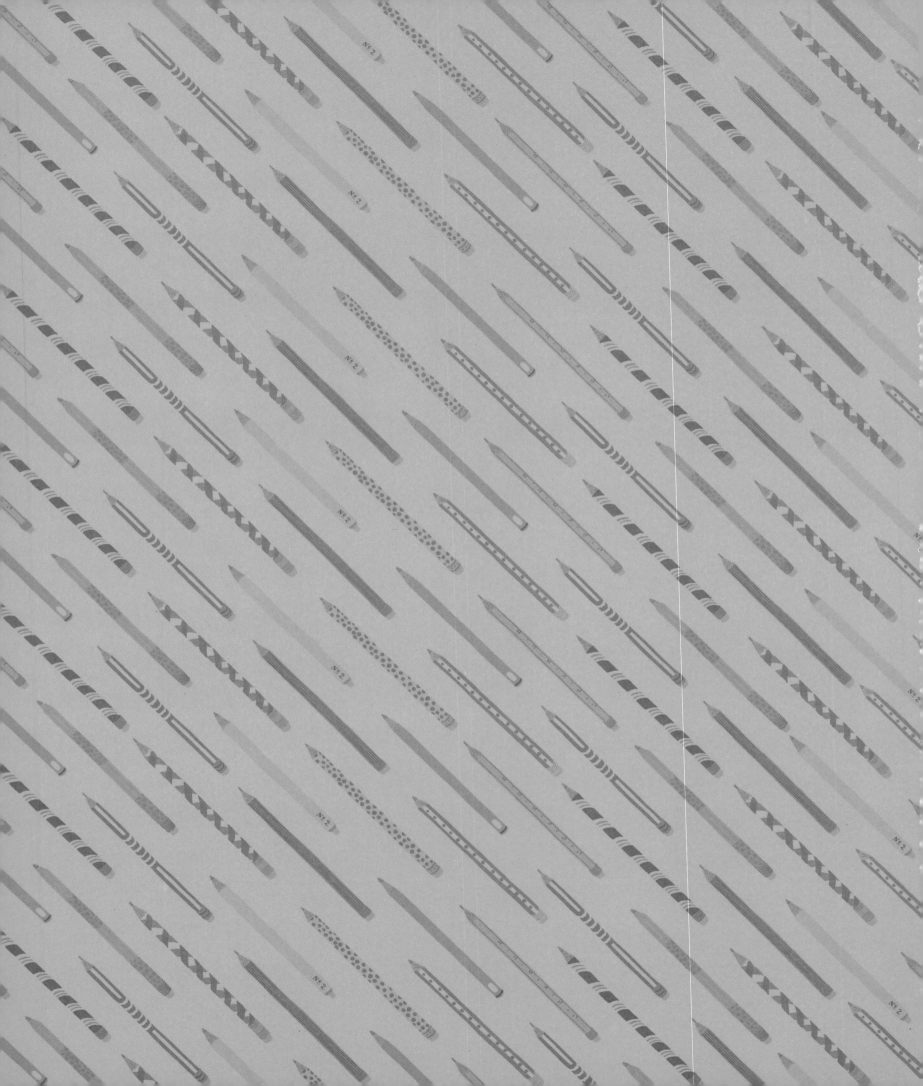